Odes About Appalachian Life

The Common Man Poetry

David Thompson

Order this book online at www.trafford.com
or email orders@trafford.com

Most Trafford titles are also available at major online book retailers.

Printed in the United States of America.

ISBN: 978-1-4669-9694-6 (sc)
ISBN: 978-1-4669-9693-9 (e)

Trafford rev. 01/09/2014

 www.trafford.com

North America & international
toll-free: 1 888 232 4444 (USA & Canada)
fax: 812 355 4082

Contents

Preface

APPALACHIANS: THE FORGOTTEN PEOPLE

Throughout the world and in our own Land people in need are cared for and lifted up as ones who need help. But the people of Appalachia are so often overlooked. Few have come to their defense about the mineral rights sold for nearly nothing to corporations and conglomerates. They stole for them because of illiteracy. Then, the Bureaucrats in charge made and make millions for themselves and corporations with no consideration for the disadvantaged Appalachian. By taking advantage of Appalachians, their esprit de corps has often been taken from them and they've withdrawn. They developed a culture of independence and a determination to live with pride. They developed a shield from the world in spite of being overlooked and have resented being looked down upon as dumb Hillbillies.

Whereas like in Oklahoma, many of the Native Americans received great rewards for the land they sold, it was not so with the Appalachian. Neither the people nor the Appalachian States received proper payment for the Coal, Gas, Oil, Salt, Sulfur and Iron extracted from their native soil. Instead there was a rape of the Appalachian Land and people have been overlooked and forgotten.

Should there not be equal attention given to poverty in Appalachia as is given to Africa and for example the Gypsies? Why raise the questions about the injustice of pay in Mexico and China and not Appalachia? And why is it the same methods used about injustice are not used for the Appalachian? What about the question and issue of fairness? Equal treatment and equal empathy should exist for Appalachia. Why do people of power not raise their voice in defense of the Appalachians? Why not have the extra mile making sure families of Appalachia receive the same missionary specialists as those in far off lands? Why does the Federal Government buy great quantities of minerals? Then, they make the wealthy wealthier by giving the wealthy deals on leases and mineral rights while the Appalachian gets no reward for the minerals taken from the soil because of not being able to read or write properly? Reparation, no! But a fair deal, yes!

Yes the corporations, the wealthy, the Government, the establishment, the prophets, and the press have neglected and overlooked the Appalachian people. The Appalachians are forgotten. Although much of the following pages may be focused on West Virginia, they reflect much of the conditions and attitudes that exist in Appalachia.

Introduction

The poems and stories attempt to raise concerns about the effects of what is happening within one's world and what is happening outside of one's world. Some of the situations are personal, some are from what others may have experienced and witnessed to and some are imaginary. The purpose of this book is to help motivate one to consider one's inward outward world.

In Self Conflict

I Can't Give in
But I Want to

I can't give in but I want to
I am cast out in all I do
I cannot work and help the crew
I cannot talk and earn my due
I cannot act and make it through
I cannot hear and get chewed
I can't give in but I want to
I am cast out in all I do

If I Could Get To Where I'm Going

If I could get to where I'm going
If I could get where wind is blowing
I know life would then be showing
If I could get to where I'm going

I've been stuck in a place not mine
Born in this world at this time
But my life here does not rhyme
And I know there's a better find

I do all that I have to do
But this life is far from true
I dream of a life that is new
Where I'm free from these blues

This world has got me down
Still, I have to stick around
I can't leave to fairer ground
Commitments keep me bound

I know it's a lot to ask for
But I hurt deep to the core
This life has become a chore
And I long for another shore

If I could get where I'm going
If I could get where wind is blowing
I know life would be showing
If I could get to where I'm going

A HILLYBILLY CONFESSION

I quietly sing and tap my foot
As music plays it taps my roots

I'm one of the Hillbilly Boys
Who's no good playing your toys

I like fishing, swimming and guns
I know exactly where I am from

The "come heres" think they are right
Still, they lack crust for a good fight

The do gooders come to our State
Using money to control our fate

But the inside rights they cannot take
The spiritual rights I won't forsake

No, I'll just listen to old hound dogs
And raise my chicken, calves, and hogs

I'm on My Way to Nashville

I'm on my way to Nashville
I'm heading there today
I'm on my way to Nashville
I'm gonna lift my gray

I've gotta hear the music
I've gotta hear that sound
I've gotta see in person
Before I'm in the ground

Is This The Way My Life Will Be?

Is this the way my life will be
Working the coal where I can't see
Confined to here and can't sail seas
Not able to see the real trees?
Is this the way life will be?

I LONG FOR THE GOOD OLD TIMES THAT WERE

I long for good old times that were
When the simple life was very clear
When there was no fear of big bear
When one was free without a fear
When friends were always really near
When regional wars were more rare
When the common good all did share

IN THE PINK

I do not think I'm in the pink
When all around this life I sink
That is connected a great link
That false is good and good's a wink
Trinkets are passed as if a mink
And lies are told without a blink
But some will say, I'm in the pink
But I know best when funds shrink
My life is filled with deep red ink

I'M READY TO FOLD

I'm ready to fold giving up the light
I cannot act and do what's right
Too many things keep me from fight
Family and culture hold to me tight
They keep me down with all their might

THE WORST OF BOTH WORLDS

One world is with a poor purse
One world is with only a hearse
One world is with no empathy
One world is with no sympathy
One world is with rare health care
One world is with no help there
One world is with pay real poor
One world is with pay in stores
One world is with little service
One world is with a dis-service
One world is with no voices
One world is with no choices
One world is with selfishness
One world is with a real mess
These two worlds are at worst
The less fortunate has been cursed

I WANTED TO LEAVE BUT I COULD NOT

I wanted to leave but I could not
Leave my culture from this spot
So as it is I will just rot
And grow old and cannot stop
My working life will not be hot
For this indeed is my own lot
I must settle for what I've got
I wanted to leave but could not

NOT BEING HOME
I AM LOST

Not being home I am lost
I miss the fun and the roast
I miss my Mom and her toast
I miss my Dad and his boast
I miss my friends, we were close
I miss my love who I love most
Not being home I am lost

UP THE HOLLOW AND STUCK HERE

Up the hollow and stuck here
Family and friends think I fear
It is true I don't think clear
But I really want to be out there
So what they have I can share

Poor and Incomplete

On a trail that's incomplete
There's no way for some replete
It always leads to a defeat
Yet I cannot now retreat
So I try and also greet
There's no such trail for elite
I am nothing when we meet

UNGLUED

I don't feel like I want to
I am tired of all of you
I don't want to make it through
I'm overwhelmed and in a stew
I guess that's why I am unglued

ALONE

No one to see, no one to care
No one to have, not one to share
No one to show, no one to dare

AN UNHAPPY APPALACHIAN

On top of nothing, all's fallen down
My whole life is a big frown
Life is not happy as is a clown
It seems I'm always on the ground
And like a dog I am in a pound

I'M AFRAID APPALACHIAN

Am I afraid, you bet I am
I'm afraid to take a stand
I'm afraid to use my hand
I'm afraid I cannot stand
I'm afraid I will have fame
I'm afraid I'll be a ham
Am I afraid you bet I am

A MIND RESISTER

I now work on but time will pass
And as it comes I'll do my task
In the meantime I take the sass
From ones with their mindless base
I hope real soon to meet the brass

An Appalachian
In Love

I'm wiped out, I'm up and down
I saw beauty without a frown
She was exquisite and not a clown
Her smile was loud with no sound
She was a queen from head to ground
I am in love and like a hound
I do believe I am heaven bound

In Desertion

NOT BOTHERING TO COME BACK

I've been down this road before
And I've been on many a track
But this time Dear
The trip is sure
I'm not bothering to come back
To see you any more

I've listened daily to your gripes
And I've heard your twisted facts
But you somehow think
Life's always ripe
I've decided to move on
I'm not bothering to come back

I've watched and tried to understand
And I have heard you what you lack

But your many words
Are not a band
I'm out of here
I'm not bothering to come back

You've walled those blue eyes at me
You've tried to make me crazy
You think my Dear I don't see
And that I am that lazy
Still I'm not bothering to come back
Even if life's hazy

I've been down this road before
And I've been on many a track
But this time Dear
The trip is sure
I'm not bothering to come back
To see you any more

THE NAGGING WOMAN LEFT BEHIND

As you look around you may find
The nagging woman I left behind
She was so rude and so unkind
And I left her in her own bind

It all started twelve months ago
With no money that I could show
Though I worked hard it did not grow
And she made those sounds like a crow

Day and night she showed no love
Then she confessed of another glove
He was one she most thought of
I then decided to give her a shove

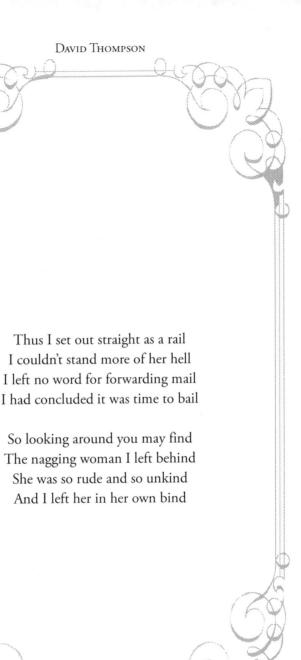

Thus I set out straight as a rail
I couldn't stand more of her hell
I left no word for forwarding mail
I had concluded it was time to bail

So looking around you may find
The nagging woman I left behind
She was so rude and so unkind
And I left her in her own bind

THE FOOD I ATE

I was doing great until I ate
The awful food upon my plate
Prepared by chefs who held my fate
Who worked to slow as food came late
And yet somehow they seem to rate

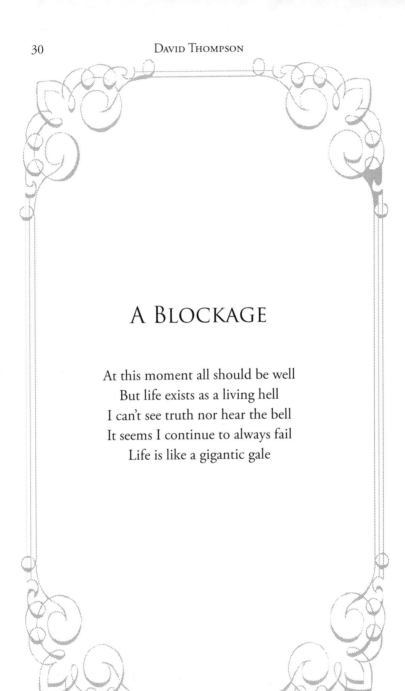

A BLOCKAGE

At this moment all should be well
But life exists as a living hell
I can't see truth nor hear the bell
It seems I continue to always fail
Life is like a gigantic gale

A KNOCK WHILE ALL ALONE

I heard a knock while all alone
It was as if one threw a stone
I dare not call by telephone
For who would listen to my tone
Instead I'm stuck in this prone
With fear and a night groan
I now wait for another home
In this world before life's gone

A COMPANION NOT A MOTHER

One rejection after another,
Makes me want to go no further.
I do indeed need another,
Who can help as no other.
But need not another mother.

AN UNRESPONDENT TO MY LOVE

She's long, lean and beautiful.
She has a style so dutiful
But there I sit so pitiful
Hoping she'll be merciful,
In this awful crucible.

WHAT ELSE IS NEW?

What else is new she said to me
She seem to want all of my tree
So I consented to a degree
But she went further than I agreed
And wanted to take what was free
I refused her shouting spree
Now she's alone and I can see

NOT MY DAY

Her innocent smile and gesturing ways
Made me think this was my day
This one of beauty lights up a way
But as it were she did not stay
For she turned out as feet of clay
Then I left to change this gray
So I could live in a spring May

NO MORE TIME
FOR YOU TO STAY

There is no more time for you to stay
You've won out, be on your way
Please move on for your own day
Leave me at peace and keep away

You left me out as clothes to dry
You stopped my empathy and why?
You shared false tears and shrill cries
You wanted more before I die

You filled my life with misery
You removed what was my tree
You made me always to agree
Now Dear be gone, for I am free

There are no tears upon my heart
So go on shopping with your cart
I will not meet you at the Mart

KNOWING ALL THE FACTS

Her eyes were green, her hair black
It was my wife who stayed on track
She always knew all the facts
She was not known for great tact
Her words would often have a smack
So I decided to take up slack
I left her there for what I lacked

How It Started

It all started sometime ago
When we went to a picture show

There we met the nicest man
Always willing to give a hand

Although new, he was real near
With me gone, he calmed her fears

He wiped away all my wife's tears
And showed how much he did care

While away, they made a plot
They would leave from our spot

Away they went as they were hot
She left me and did not stop

DON'T WAIT FOR ME

Don't wait for me I won't be home
I'm tired of gripes and now I'm gone
All that you did was pick a bone
Even when you used the phone
I now want to be left alone

IN HER BED

There she lies in her bed
I just want to kiss her head

She's the one who has heart
Full of grace at every start

She's the one that I loved
The only one who's a dove

A lovely lady full of grace
With her love I could face

I wanted near in her space
And I could win any race

But she left me for another
For someone like a brother

My work took me far away
But he was there with his say

Soon all talk got real close
She thought he was a great host

She then moved to another bed
And I almost lost my head

Though we are now far apart
She still remains in my heart

DOWN AND OUT

I'm down and out and I feel bad
I lost my wife and I've been had
She seemed to think life was too sad
And left me here as the new fad
The end result she was real glad

Now I stay at home alone
I want no calls by telephone
My heart breaks with silent tones
And I hurt right to the bone
Yet I hope she's forever gone

DID YOU EVER FEEL SHAFTED?

Did you ever feel shafted, did you ever feel bad
Did you ever feel lonely, did you ever feel had
I can't speak for you but life is unsure
I've lost everything and can't find a cure

Well I've wasted my life in working this place
I've spent too much time in this awful race
I worked hard for years working the floor
The boss just informed me my job is no more

I've got me a daughter in college just now
I can't pay her bills I must tell her somehow
My wife, she is sick with a cancerous sore
Which stopped our vacation I've cancelled our tour

I'm telling you Buddy this world is a pain
Tear drops keep falling just like the rain
I'd end this old life were not for my kin
I almost don't care, I'm in a tail spin

Did you ever felt shafted, did you ever feel bad
Did you ever feel lonely, did you ever feel had
I can't speak for you but life seems unsure
I've lost everything and can't find a cure

In Contemplation

OPPORTUNITIES

All kinds of time to do one's thing
All kinds of openings to make life sing
All kinds of help that has a ring
All kinds of love that helps one cling
All kinds of faith that makes one fling
All kinds of light that gives one wings
All kinds of time to do one's thing

NOT SATISFIED

Not satisfied the way things are
Not satisfied about my cares

Not satisfied in what I see
Not satisfied the way things be

Not satisfied with truth and fact
Not satisfied there are some cracks

Not satisfied in what I give
Not satisfied the way I live

Not satisfied in what I know
Not satisfied in what I show

Not satisfied with what's beyond
Not satisfied life's now all gone

WHY?

Why am I sore about what is?
Why can't I grasp what all gives?
Why is it I'm in a 'tiz?
Why has life become a fizz?
Perhaps I do not like the quiz?

I WOULD MISS IT
BUT I WON'T

I would miss it but I won't
Leave this place, all say don't
They say stay with their taunts
And cling to me with the wants
I could leave but I shan't

MOVING TOWARD PEACE

Let us begin with some compromise
Let us be clear with no surprise
Let us then work with no disguise
Let us agree to have no lies
Let us shake hands without dark skies

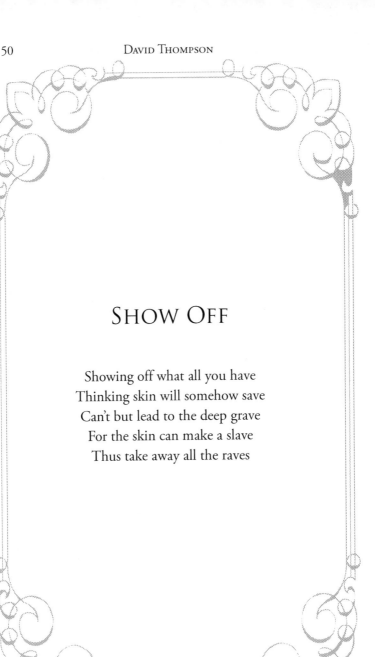

SHOW OFF

Showing off what all you have
Thinking skin will somehow save
Can't but lead to the deep grave
For the skin can make a slave
Thus take away all the raves

THE YOUNG AND YOUNG

The young and young do not grow old
They stay with life until it folds
Their life is like pure solid gold
They're on the move and always bold
They do not stop though some scold

WORLDLY HERALDS

In the throes of a war-torn world
When some yell they're real heralds
Be careful what may then unfurl
For you could end up in a barrel
With a future that's in a swirl

MENTAL EXERCISE

Alone amid noise and people
I am inspired by this steeple

I contemplate about what's not
Something appears right on the spot

And I wonder about my lot
There's no time for sleepy cots

For if I stop I know I'll rot
And I'll develop one big pot

Alone with noise and people
I am inspired by this steeple

IF I COULD SAY BUT ONE GOOD WORD

If I could say but one good word
How would I want the word heard?

Would I be loud for all to hear?
Would I speak soft for those near?

Would I use words with none to spare?
Would I punctuate and make a spear?

Would I want all to have a share?
Would I want words with a care?

If I could say but one good word
How would I want the word heard?

PARADOX OF THOUGHT

Are thoughts I think all my own
Or is there something beyond home

I think it is, but then I don't
I think I will and then I won't

I don't want to but I'm boxed
In this condition I can't out fox

Below and Above Spheres

Down below and up above
Are the spheres where I am shoved

There us my love who I so love
But there's another who I can't have

One sphere is real, the other less
Yet both exist I must confess

A Moving Light Unexplained

A moving light was glowing green
The fastest light I'd ever seen
I could hardly catch the scene

Was I blessed with my naked eye?
Here all alone I did try
It could outrun even the sky

The smartest ones who know so much
Seems that they had run amok
And were filled with a quiet hush

The thingified could not catch this
As they wondered just what is
While some were left in a 'tiz?

THE RE-ORDERING OF ONE'S TIME

The re-ordering of one's time
May be done on a dime
But one can't always define
Although walking in a line
There are times that do not rhyme

AMBIGUITY EXISTS

An ambiguity exists, life is vague
I'm overwhelmed and cannot save

This may take me to the grave
For deep within I am not brave

I seek out friends who I know
But satisfaction does not glow

I try institutions for some relief
But disappointment brings more grief

What is the answer to this condition
Am I a child of the perdition?

WHILE

I

While the days are clear,
While life is good,
While money's there,
While understood,
While time is fair,
While in the mood,
It's time to share

II

While you have one,
While you have friends,
While you have sun,
While you have wind,
While you can run,
While you can tend,
Your must not shun

THE GOOD OLD DAYS

Some want to find
The good days of old
When eggs were a dime
And workers were told
They would be fined
Or dig more coal
In spite of the grim
When they had colds
And live on brine
In the winters' cold
It hurt to spine
Yet one would scold
To get moonshine
Or go past mold
On the outhouse sign
O some had gold
From the deep mine
They had a hold
And a hostile mind
And could be bold
To the ones that signed

QUESTION OF ONE'S CULTURE

Is one's own culture
Also a vulture
that keeps one captive
From being free
Such a load
Keeps one off roads

PLOTTING TO MAKE THE INNOCENT GUILTY

Plotting to make the innocent guilty is what some really do
It is a tool the guilty use to make the innocent stew
They say the innocent are overpaid while working as a crew
They say the innocent are to blame when profits don't
come through
They say the innocent use the banks but fail to use their cue
They say the innocent have health bills that make them
all turn blue
They say the innocent use the war to make their dreams
come true
Plotting to make the innocent guilty is what some really do
It is a tool the guilty use to make the innocent stew

DREAM WOMAN

One day I saw one like a queen
In stylish pink, she made a scene

She walked as on a clear mission
With exact strides and no omissions

Her dark brown hair shined in the sun
It seemed so clear that she could run

Her white shoe heels were one inch high
And as she walked I could see the sky

She smiled at all who passed her by
Oh I tell you I wanted to fly

She headed toward the local store
And it was obvious she was no bore

Out came a list from her pocketbook
It was real long and the food she took!

She called a cab to take her home
It was clear she was there alone

I said to her, "Please let me help.
On this hot day you'll surely wilt.

I have my car around the corner
It's air conditioned and I'm the owner."

My face got red at my boldness
But it didn't matter about my oldness

With queenly grace she said, "Would you?
This food's for poor to help them through."

Believe it or not, I knew right there
Old or young I would marry her

So off we went in my new car
What others thought, I did not care

We then stopped at a family home
To visit children and a mother alone

At least for now they'd have some food
Which came from one who was so good

I asked if I could leave her off
"Why sure", she said, "I'll get my stuff."

Off we went up to her own place
To her home that was full of grace

I said goodbye, she said, "Come again!"
I knew I'd found more than a friend.

Visions of Hon

I saw a vision of my Hon
There on a rock with little on
Her legs just right and arms so strong
Her lovely smile touched my bones
Then I fell in the old pond
With every stitch of clothing on
Without a chance to even yawn
I still see her but she has gone
While I wait here in a prone
I do hope she will come home
So I'll no longer be alone

A West Virginia Vista

Looking at this vista and all that I could see
It was as if heaven had finally now touched me

I saw a clear blue sky, not a cloud to behold
I saw nature's world both young and the old

I saw cattle on a hillside
And a horse that one could ride

I saw an eagle flying high
Which caused me to just sigh

I saw a deer running far away
And a mountain lion stalking a prey

I saw the streams like living water
Filled with fish and the otter

I saw wind blowing green grass
And silent concerts with its brass

O the things of this vista scene
I must tell all where I have been

THE PEOPLE OF
WEST VIRGINIA

In the hills of West Virginia live a people
that I know best.
They are humble family people in a place
you will find rest.
They may not talk the way you want in this State
that is so blessed.
They may miss the courtly manners but they are
country I confess.
They will help out neighbors without a word
at their behest.
They are some who are bent over farming from
mountain's crest.
They are folks with great music, learned from their
mother's breast.
They are people full of goodness, they have met
all of the tests.
So come on see West Virginia and meet the people
I know the best.

In Faith

Locked in World of Powerful Sin

Locked in a world of powerful sin
There is a way out of the bin
Wrath and death may kick your shin
But One frees where you have been
His name is Jesus Whom God did send
He gave His life so you could win
He made new life to start again
Praise be to God there'll be no skin
In Heaven's gate there'll be no end.

EVALUATION OF A SERVANT

Have I seen all I could see?
Have I been all I could be?

Have I shared all I could share?
Have I heard all I could hear?

Have I walked all I could walk?
Have I talked all I could talk?

Have I loved all I could love?
Have I shoved all I could shove?

Have I saved all I could save?
Have I shaved all I could shave?

Have I felt all I could feel?
Have I healed all I could heal?

Who's to judge if one's done all?
Only God can make that call.

UNREVEALED MYSTERIES

So many mysteries unrevealed
Appeared to be somehow sealed

Blocked from truth we do not know
No matter how we make a show

Some hidden truths can be proven
But are questioned when uneven

Truth alone must be complete
Else the truth cannot compete

There can't be ambiguous truth
Else it is of little worth

Knowledge of truth beyond our scope
Cannot be part of the human crop

Still the vision contemplation
Gives in part an explanation.

A Praying Person

I really want off and away
So I can go kneel and pray
In the privacy of my day
Only God knows what I'll say
I pray God will change my gray

THE END

There is no thought, there is no word
There is no sight, there is no sword

There is silence, the dead can't hear
All is now gone, from life so dear

This all must be the final end
One cannot find even a friend

Nothing is saved in the gray grave
The time has lost to now be brave

But God can see in eternity
And God alone will set some free

THIS CYCLE

From life to death and life again
In a cycle one can't win
Yes, some say because of sin
They may wonder who'll enter in
We can't judge but our God can

PEERING

Ever so often an image appears
Partly revealed yet I still peer
All of the image is not clear
It's like the wind causing a stir
Although it's there, there is no fear
I rather think that God is near

A PLEA TO GOD

God make me new in this world
For I want to be Your herald

My desire is to live for You
For You alone make life true

QUIET BUT NOT ALONE

One cannot feel one's all alone
And endure upon one's own
For one needs those loving tones
Sometimes near and sometimes roams
Touching one before life's gone

Moved By Something

What is it that moves within?
Is it God's Spirit as a friend?
Is it a passion that won't bend?
Is it truth like the wind?
Is it something I must win?
What is it that I must tend?
What is it that moves within?

WALKING IN THE LIGHT OF JESUS

Walking in the Light of Jesus
Walking in the Light of God's Word
Walking in the Light of Jesus
Walking in the Light I've heard

He changed my life around
And new life in Him I've found
He took all my sins away
And He gave to me a new day

He has made life new that's old
He has brought me to the Fold
He has turned me from this world
He has made me His own herald

His truth has taken life's shame
And nothing is ever the same
I'm now living in His frame
And trying to help the lame

Walking in the Light of Jesus
Walking in the Light of God's Word
Walking in the Light of Jesus
Walking in the Light I've heard

INFINITE BEYOND ALL MEASURE

Infinitely infinite beyond all measure
Though we try to find the treasure
We often miss Creator's feature
And re-arrange what is the future
That's perhaps Creator's leisure
We are but one limited creature
And this may be Creator's pleasure

CHAOS AND ORDER

Chaos appears, then order comes
Interconnected like a hum
Stays in place like the sun
It's Creator's joyous fun
Chaos appears, then order comes

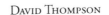

A PACIFIST

O my God, O my Lord!
I thank You that I heard,
What in truth was Your Word.
I gave up on my sword.
O my God, O my Lord!